The Life Cycle
of a
PELICAN

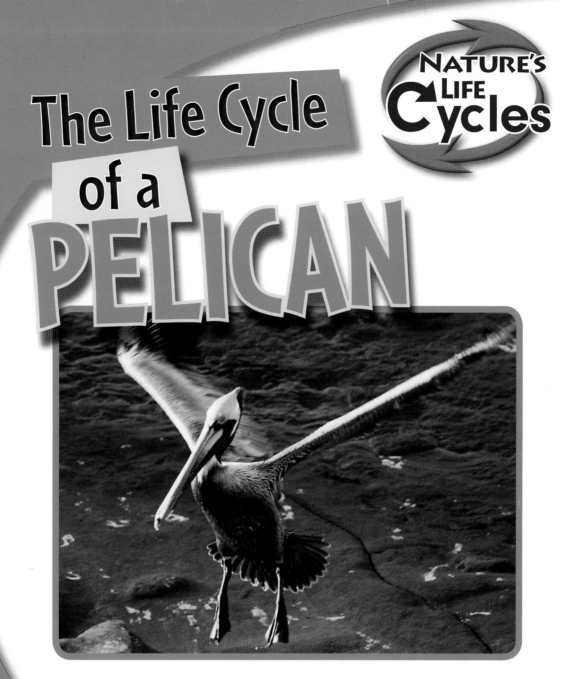

By Anna Kingston

Gareth Stevens
Publishing

Please visit our Web site, www.garethstevens.com. For a free color catalog of all our high-quality books, call toll free 1-800-542-2595 or fax 1-877-542-2596.

Library of Congress Cataloging-in-Publication Data

Kingston, Anna.
 The life cycle of a pelican / Anna Kingston.
    p. cm. – (Nature's life cycles)
 Includes bibliographical references and index.
 ISBN 978-1-4339-4684-4 (pbk. : alk. paper)
 ISBN 978-1-4339-4685-1 (6-pack)
 ISBN 978-1-4339-4683-7 (library binding : alk. paper)
 1. Pelicans—Life cycles—Juvenile literature. I. Title.
 QL696.P47K56 2011
 598.4'3156–dc22

                                        2010030692

First Edition

Published in 2011 by
Gareth Stevens Publishing
111 East 14th Street, Suite 349
New York, NY 10003

Copyright © 2011 Gareth Stevens Publishing

Designer: Daniel Hosek
Editor: Therese Shea

Photo credits: Cover, pp. 1, 4 David McNew/Getty Images; pp. 5, 7 (all images), 9 (both images), 11, 15, 17, 19, 21 (juvenile and adult) Shutterstock.com; pp. 13, 21 (egg and chick) Gail Shumway/ Photographer's Choice/Getty Images.

Printed in the United States of America

CPSIA compliance information: Batch #CW11GS: For further information contact Gareth Stevens, New York, New York at 1-800-542-2595.

Contents

Words in the glossary appear in **bold** type the first time they are used in the text.

Meet the Pelican

Pelicans are big birds that live near water. Pelicans use their beaks to catch food. The bottom part of a pelican's long beak has a pouch of stretchy skin. When it's time to eat, a pelican scoops up a mouthful of fish and water. A pelican's pouch can hold around 3 gallons (11 l) of water! Next, the pelican tips its head back. The water flows out. Then, the pelican swallows its food. Pelicans also scoop up and swallow other small water animals, such as shrimp.

AWESOME ANIMAL!

The Australian pelican has the world's longest beak.

A pelican's beak
can be as long as
20 inches (51 cm)!
▼

Getting Around

Pelicans have big bodies, long necks, large wings, and short legs. They don't walk well.

Pelicans are excellent fliers. They have hollow bones. They also have air pockets inside their bodies. These features make pelicans light. They often drift on air currents. They **flap** their big wings with long, slow strokes.

Pelicans are great swimmers. They have webbed feet. This means they have skin between their toes to help them paddle through water.

AWESOME ANIMAL!

Pelicans in a flock usually fly in a line, but they sometimes form a V shape.

Pelicans move most
easily in air or water.

Where They Live

Pelicans live on every **continent** except Antarctica. There are several **species** of pelicans. Brown pelicans live along the North American coasts of the Atlantic Ocean and Pacific Ocean. American white pelicans spend the winters along these coasts, too. In the summer, they **migrate** to inland lakes. This is where baby American white pelicans start their lives.

AWESOME ANIMAL!

The biggest pelican is the Dalmatian pelican of eastern Europe and Asia. It measures more than 10 feet (3 m) from one wingtip to the other.

American white pelican

brown pelican

All pelicans live near water so they can find plenty of tasty fish to eat!
▼

Finding a Mate

When it's time to build nests and lay eggs, pelicans gather in groups called colonies. Pelicans build their nests on the ground or in bushes and trees. They gather branches, feathers, and grass to make nests. They usually build them close together.

When male pelicans are ready to choose **mates**, they may grow colorful feathers. Pelicans **court** their mates. Sometimes they bow and fly around. Sometimes they fill their pouches with air to show off their bright orange color.

This male pelican's colorful feathers and beak will attract a mate.
▼

AWESOME ANIMAL!

American white pelicans grow a hornlike bump on their beaks when it's time to mate. The bump disappears after mating.

Eggs

Mother pelicans most often lay one to four eggs each year. Both mother and father pelicans care for their eggs. The parents keep watch for animals that eat eggs, such as skunks and raccoons. Many pelicans choose to build nests on islands where it's harder for **predators** to reach them.

Pelican parents use their big webbed feet to warm the eggs. They also use their feathers. After about 30 days, the chicks **hatch**.

AWESOME ANIMAL!

Pelicans sometimes share their nesting colonies with other water birds, such as flamingos and cormorants.

Pelican eggs have thick shells, so the weight of the parent won't break them. ▼

Chicks

Newly hatched pelican chicks can't swim, find food, or fly. The chicks don't even have feathers! They curl up next to their mother or father to stay warm. After about 10 days, the chicks grow soft feathers called down.

Pelican parents bring their chicks food. In the beginning, the parents **regurgitate**, or throw up, fish into the nest for the chicks to eat. Older pelican chicks stick their beaks into their parents' throats to get the regurgitated fish. Chicks love these meals!

A group of pelican chicks is called a pod or gang.

Juveniles and Adults

As pelican chicks grow older, they begin to walk. They learn to swim. By the time they're between 9 and 12 weeks old, they become "fully fledged." This means that they have all the feathers they need to fly.

The young birds are now called **juveniles**. Juveniles watch older pelicans fishing to learn to fish themselves. Pelicans have a full coat of adult feathers when they're about 3 years old. This is around the age they begin to mate.

AWESOME ANIMAL!

Most pelicans live to be about 15 years old. Some live as long as 30 years!

Juveniles leave their nest to find other young pelicans. ▼

Fishing for a Meal

Different species of pelicans fish in different ways. Brown pelicans fly high over the water. When they spot fish, they dive down and scoop them up.

American white pelicans dip their heads into the water for a meal. Sometimes they work together to drive fish to shallow water. There, the fish are easier to catch.

All pelicans drain the water from their pouches before eating. Other water birds may steal the pelican's fish while the water is draining. Some even land on the pelican's head!

Some pelicans grab fish under the water. Plants in the water help the pelican hide.

19

Protecting Pelicans

In the past, people hunted pelicans for their feathers. Fishermen killed pelicans because they feared the birds ate too many fish. However, some people wanted to **protect** pelicans. In 1903, President Theodore Roosevelt made Florida's Pelican Island a wildlife **refuge**.

The 2010 Gulf of Mexico oil spill killed many pelicans. When oil covers their feathers, they can't fly or swim. It also causes pelican eggs to break easily. Hopefully, places like Pelican Island can help save these beautiful birds from similar events.

The Life Cycle of a Pelican

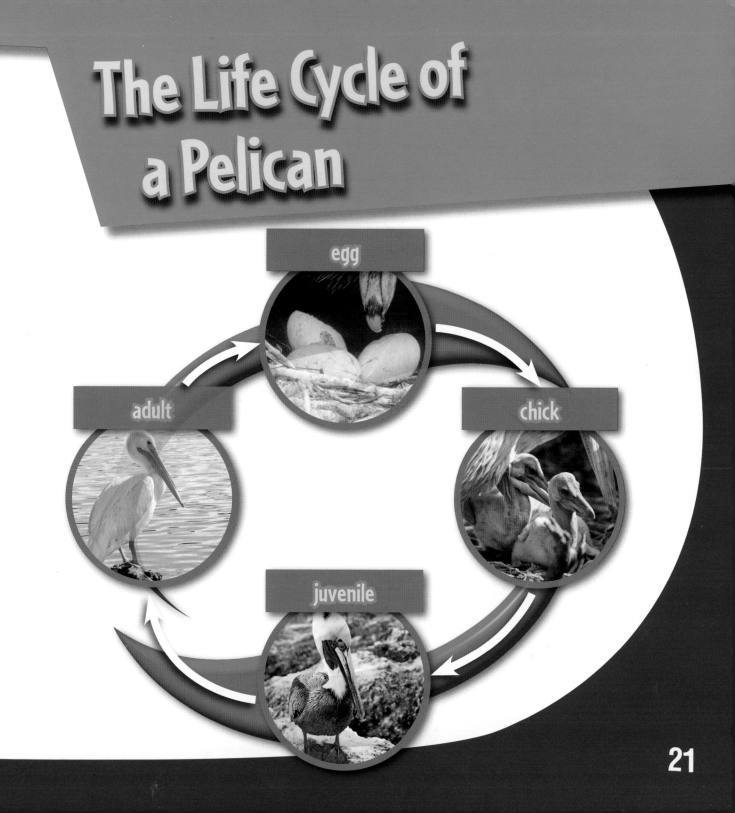

egg

chick

adult

juvenile

Glossary

continent: one of Earth's seven large landmasses

court: to try to gain another's interest

flap: to move up and down or back and forth

hatch: to come out of an egg

juvenile: a bird that is older than a chick and younger than an adult

mate: one of two animals that come together to make babies

migrate: to move from one place to another

predator: an animal that kills other animals for food

protect: to keep safe

refuge: a place set aside for wild animals to live safely

regurgitate: to throw up partly eaten food

species: one kind of living thing. All people are one species.

For More Information

Books

Cussen, Sarah. *Those Peculiar Pelicans*. Sarasota, FL: Pineapple Press, 2005.

Halfmann, Janet. *Pelican's Catch*. Norwalk, CT: Soundprints, 2004.

Stout, Frankie. *Pelicans: Soaring the Seas*. New York, NY: PowerKids Press, 2008.

Web Sites

Birds: Pelican
www.sandiegozoo.org/animalbytes/t-pelican.html
Read fun facts about several pelican species.

Pelican
animals.nationalgeographic.com/animals/birds/pelican
See a map of pelicans around the world. Hear sounds that pelicans make.

Index